This book
belongs to

Published 2016 by Kitaab Cellar

First published in Great Britain in 2013 by Greenbird Books
Text © 2013 by Aisha Mohammed & Sajida Mohammed
Illustrations © 2013 by Azra Momin

ISBN 978-1533255884

With love and deep appreciation,
Mama and Baba.

It was time for the monthly cake sale at school, Safiyyah was very excited. She had spotted a really scrummy, delicious looking chocolate cake.

'Mama, can you give me some money to buy that chocolate cake please?' she asked politely.

Her mother smiled, 'Of course, how much is it?'
'It's one pound Mama,' said Safiyyah.

So her mother gave her a big shiny two pound coin. 'Jazakallah Mama!' she beamed, handing the coin to the friendly woman behind the stall.

'Jazakallah,' the woman said with a big smile on her face. 'Enjoy your cake!'

'Wa Iyyaki,' Safiyyah replied, 'I will Insha'Allah.'

'Safiyyah, why don't we leave the change with the lady for Sadaqah?' suggested her mother.

Safiyyah looked down at her shiny pound coin, she didn't want to give it away.

'No Mama, I don't want to give it...'

'Do you know what Sadaqah is?' asked her mother.

'No, Mama I don't know, what is Sadaqah?'

'Let's go home and talk about it with Baba after Maghrib Insha'Allah.'

When Baba got home that evening, Safiyyah, her younger brother Ibrahim and little sister Aaminah were very happy to see him.

The house was full of smiles with lots of hugs and kisses to go round.

'We missed you Baba,' Safiyyah said.

'I missed you too, little ones,' said Baba.

It was the family's favourite time of day, especially baby Ibrahim, who was just learning to talk.

After Maghrib, Safiyyah's mother took Ibrahim and Aaminah to bed.

It was Baba's turn to read to Safiyyah, this evening he had a special story to tell.

'I am going to teach you about Sadaqah. Our beloved prophet, may Allah's peace and blessings be upon him, taught us to give to those who have less than us. He reminded us, that every act of kindness is Sadaqah. Even smiling at your brother and sister is Sadaqah,' said Baba.

'I smiled at the lady today, was that Sadaqah Baba?'

'Yes it was Safiyyah and Insha'Allah you will be greatly rewarded for it. Our good deeds will help us, but some good deeds will help us a long time after we return to Allah.'

'Like Nana's good deed! I miss Nana very much,' sighed Safiyyah.

'We all miss Nana very much. But Nana did something very special in her lifetime, she helped build our Masjid.

Allah has told us,

*Who ever builds a Masjid for Allah, Allah will Build for him a similar House in Paradise**

Nana will receive a reward for each prayer that is made in the Masjid she helped build. The rewards are for Nana Insha'Allah and will continue!'

Safiyyah closed her eyes and imagined a beautiful Masjid. She felt very happy knowing Nana was getting lots of reward.

'What can I do Baba to get a reward?'

'We will make a Jariyah Jar Safiyyah! This is what I did with my Baba when I was young like you. A Jariyah Jar is like a special money box. All the money you save in it will go to charity. Tomorrow is Friday, after school we will begin.'

SADAQAH JARIYA

Friday was a very special day and Safiyyah and her siblings were always given extra special treats.

Safiyyah was very excited about making her Jariya Jar.

'Look Baba, Mama gave me a jar we could use! I can save my Sadaqah money in here. We can call it Safiyyah's Jariya Jar!'

Baba was very pleased with Safiyyah and her wonderful idea.

Baba and Safiyyah spent the rest of the evening cutting and sticking.

They used lots of special paper, colouring pens and stickers to make the Jariya Jar.

When they had finished, Baba said:

'I'm very proud of you Safiyyah, you have really made a beautiful Jariya Jar, may Allah reward you for your intentions.'

'But Baba, where do I get intentions from? I have never seen them!'

'Intentions come from your heart Safiyyah, they are your true feelings. When you wanted to make this Jariya Jar your true feeling was to save up your money to give to Sadaqah. Allah will reward you for these true feelings.'

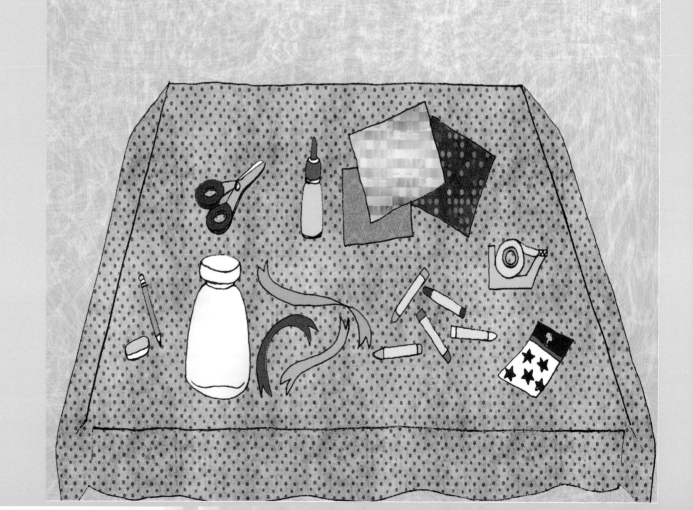

After all the excitement, Safiyyah was very tired. She thought for a moment about everything her Baba had told her.

'Baba can you put my shiny pound coin in my Jariya Jar, I want to give it to someone who needs it more than I do.'

'Yes of course I can.' Baba gave Safiyyah a very big hug and tucked her into bed.

Safiyyah now really understood the importance of Sadaqah. That night, after Safiyyah said her duas she went to sleep extremely happy.

She even dreamt of her Jariya Jar and all the beautiful intentions she had growing inside them.

Kitaab Cellar

Printed in Great Britain
by Amazon